THE ULTIMATE CHRISTMAS QUIZ BOOK

Kate & Steve Haywood

Copyright © 2021 Kate & Steve Haywood

All rights reserved.

Table of Contents

Introduction 7

Celebrity Christmas Birthdays 9

Christmas Missing Vowels 11

Christmas Food 13

Christmas Reindeer 15

Christmas Chronology 17

Christmas Films 19

Christmas Jokes (1) 21

Christmas Anagrams 23

Christmas True or False 25

Trivia - Christmas Trees at the White House 27

Christmas Songs 29

Christmas Books 31

Playing Santa 33

Favourite Pantomime Characters 35

Bestselling Christmas Toys 37

Christmas History 39

Lyrics From Christmas Songs 41

Christmas Geography 43

Who Am I? (1) 45

Christmas Pot Luck	47
Christmas Carol Initials	49
Christmas Word Ladder (1)	51
Christmas Jokes (2)	53
Christmas Games	55
Christmas Colours	57
Christmas TV Specials	59
Who Am I? (2)	61
Christmas Nativity	63
The Twelve Days of Christmas	65
Christmas Word Ladder (2)	67
Santa by Any Other Name	69
Christmas No. 1's	71
Christmas Missing Vowels (2)	73
Name the Film By the Stars	75
Christmas Trivia - Crackers	77
Winter Sports	79
Who Am I? (3)	81
Name the Christmas Item	83
Christmas Tipples	85
A Little Latin Christmas	87
Christmas Trivia - Mince Pies	89

Mince Pie Recipe 91
Christmas Trivia - Song Royalties 93
Post-Christmas Trivia (1) 95
Post-Christmas Trivia (2) 97
Post-Christmas Trivia (3) 99
Post-Christmas Trivia (4) 101
Post-Christmas Trivia (5) 103
Post-Christmas Link Words 105

Introduction

Welcome to our Christmas Quiz Book made to make Christmas go off with a bang.

This book has easy navigation. At the beginning of the book is a table of contents which directs you to each quiz, so you can either pick and choose or read through the quizzes one by one. The quizzes all appear on the right-hand pages, with the answers directly afterwards, over the page on the left hand side. In that way, you can easily navigate between quizzes and answers, but can't see the answers before you're ready to check them.

We hope you enjoy this quiz book. If you like it, please consider writing a review! We've also written other quiz books for your enjoyment (or they make good stocking fillers!), just search for us on Amazon. Thank you!

If you enjoy our quizzes, take a look at our Facebook page - https://www.facebook.com/quiziclebooks. We regularly post quizzes, trivia and other fun content as well as details about new quiz books we've got coming out. Also check out our website at www.quiziclebooks.com and subscribe to our mailing list to get a free subscribers quiz book!

HAPPY CHRISTMAS!

Celebrity Christmas Birthdays

Can you guess these celebrities with 25th December birthdays?

1. British singer-songwriter, she has won more Brit Awards than any other female artist, has performed at the closing ceremony of the London 2012 Olympics and won an academy award for her soundtrack to The Lord of the Rings: The Return of the King movie.
2. English scientist, born in 1642, he is one of the inventors of calculus and his most famous work is Principia Mathematica.
3. American actress who played Carrie in the 1976 film of the same name.
4. Sister of famous English poet, she posthumously became famous in her own right for her Lake District journals.
5. American actor, married to actress Lauren Bacall, and star of The Maltese Falcon, Casablanca, The Big Sleep and African Queen plus many more.
6. Born in 1971, this Canadian Prime Minister was also the son of a Prime Minister.
7. British chef, she was the winner of BBC's The Great British Bake Off in 2015.
8. English singer born in 1971 whose birth name was Florian Cloud de Bounevialle Armstrong. Her brother was part of the British group Faithless.
9. English writer whose most famous work was The Naked Civil Servant. Sting's song 'An Englishman in New York' was written about this person.
10. Irish singer and musician who fronted the pop band The Pogues, famous for Fairytale of New York.

Answers - Celebrity Christmas Birthdays

1. Annie Lennox
2. Isaac Newton
3. Sissy Spacek
4. Dorothy Wordsworth
5. Humphry Bogart
6. Justin Trudeau
7. Nadiya Hussain
8. Dido
9. Quentin Crisp
10. Shane MacGowan

Christmas Missing Vowels

Can you find the missing vowels in these sets of consonants and create Christmas themed words?

1. CHRSTMS CRCKR
2. MNC PS
3. RST PTTS
4. SNT CLS
5. MLLD WN
6. PPR HT
7. RD CBBG
8. PRSNTS
9. VGRN TR
10. GGNG
11. TRKY
12. FRNKNCNS
13. YL LG
14. PNSTT
15. BBLS

Answers - Christmas Missing Vowels

1. Christmas cracker
2. Mince Pies
3. Roast Potatoes
4. Santa Claus
5. Mulled Wine
6. Paper Hat
7. Red Cabbage
8. Presents
9. Evergreen Tree
10. Eggnog
11. Turkey
12. Frankincense
13. Yule Log
14. Poinsettia
15. Baubles

Christmas Food

Can you answer these Christmas food questions from around the world?

1. Swedish Julgröt and Icelandic Möndlugrautur are Christmas rice puddings with what kind of nut hidden in the centre?
2. Panforte, Panettone and Pandoro are popular Christmas cakes in which country?
3. What popular Christmas food is translated from English variously as gjeldeti, tacchino, kuleke and dundjan
4. Which food poisoning bacteria is often prevalent in homemade Eggnog due to the typical treatment of one of the ingredients?
5. White Christmas is a sweet treat made from ingredients including raisins, glace cherries and desiccated coconut, bound with hydrogenated coconut oil. In which country is it popular?
6. Which two European countries produce the most Brussels sprouts (they both produce around the same amount annually)?
7. In *A Christmas Carol* by Charles Dickens, which bird does Scrooge see Bob Cratchit's family eating with the Ghost of Christmas Present, and which bird does he buy the Cratchit's at the end of the book
8. What fun name is given to sausages wrapped in bacon?
9. What is the name of the spongy, honey-sweetened spicy German biscuit, popular around Christmas?
10. Turron is popular in Spain, Puerto Rico and Cuba over Christmas, but what kind of sweet is it?

Answers - Christmas Food

1. Almond
2. Italy
3. Turkey
4. Salmonella (if uncooked egg yolks are used)
5. Australia
6. The Netherlands (Holland) and the United Kingdom (Great Britain)
7. He sees them eating a goose (a typical Christmas bird at this time) and he buys them a turkey (a very exotic bird at this time)
8. Pigs in blankets
9. Lebkuchen
10. Nougat

Christmas Reindeer

Can you name all of Santa's reindeer? There are nine of them, eight originals and one more modern inclusion.

For a bonus point, can you name (and have a guess at the date) of the literary work which first mentions the reindeer by name?

Answers - Christmas Reindeer

Santa's Reindeer are:
Dasher, Dancer, Prancer, Vixen, Comet, Cupid, Donner, Blitzen and Rudolph.

The first eight reindeer appeared for the first time in the Clement C. Moore poem *A Visit From St Nicholas* or as it is often known, *The Night Before Christmas* from 1823. Here is an extract from the poem:

"When, what to my wondering eyes should appear,
but a miniature sleigh, and eight tiny rein-deer,
with a little old driver, so lively and quick,
I knew in a moment it must be St. Nick.

More rapid than eagles his coursers they came,
And he whistled, and shouted, and call'd them by name:
"Now, Dasher! Now, Dancer! Now, Prancer, and Vixen!
"On, Comet! On, Cupid! On, Dunder and Blixem!

"To the top of the porch! to the top of the wall!
"Now dash away! dash away! dash away all!"
As dry leaves that before the wild hurricane fly,
When they meet with an obstacle, mount to the sky;

So up to the house-top the coursers they flew"
Dunder and Blitzen eventually became Donner and Blitzen, which is actually German for Thunder and Lightning.
Rudolph came later, in a verse written by Robert L May for a department store which included it in a book for children.

Christmas Chronology

Put these sets of three festive themed events in date order.

1) **Christmas Tunes of the 1950s**
    a) *Blue Christmas* first appears on *Elvis' Christmas Songs* Album
    b) *Santa Baby* is originally recorded by Eartha Kitt
    c) *Christmas Alphabet* is released by Dickie Valentine and is the ever first chart topper to be actually about Christmas

2) **Events on Christmas Day**
    a) 7.6 magnitude earthquake occurs in Qansu, China killing 275 people
    b) Ringo Star of Beatles fame, receives his first ever drum kit
    c) Legendary 'Christmas Truce' takes place between British and German Troops who play football and exchange gifts

3) **New Year**
    a) The oldest known sparkling wine was created
    b) Auld Lang Syne was written
    c) Use of fireworks are first documented.

Answers - Christmas Chronology

Here is the correct order.

1) **Christmas Tunes of the 1950s**
   a) *Santa Baby* is originally recorded by Eartha Kitt (1953)
   b) *Christmas Alphabet* is released by Dickie Valentine and is the ever first chart topper to be actually about Christmas (1955)
   c) *Blue Christmas* first appears on *Elvis' Christmas Songs* Album (1957)

2) **Events on Christmas Day**
   a) Legendary 'Christmas Truce' takes place between British and German Troops who play football and exchange gifts (1914)
   b) 7.6 magnitude earthquake occurs in Qansu, China killing 275 people (1932)
   c) Ringo Star of Beatles fame, receives his first ever drum kit (1959)

3) **New Year**
   a) Use of fireworks documented (c. 7th century, China)
   b) The oldest known sparkling wine is created (1531)
   c) Auld Lang Syne is written (1788

Christmas Films

Try out these questions all about Christmassy films

1. In what decade did *It's a Wonderful Life* hit the big screen?
2. In *The Nightmare Before Christmas* which character abducts Santa Claus?
3. The film *White Christmas* starred Christmas favourite Bing Crosby but who composed the music and lyrics?
4. Which original song does Billy Mack change the words to, resulting in a Christmas number one, in *Love Actually*?
5. Who plays main character Buddy in *Elf*?
6. *8 Women* is a film about a murder at Christmastime, but from what country does the film originate?
7. *The Muppets Christmas Carol* is a popular one at this time of year, but who created The Muppets?
8. The film *Last Christmas* is a 2019 romantic comedy based around music from which British pop group?
9. In the reimagining of a classic, Bill Murray plays the main character in *Scrooged*, but how many of his brothers also appear in the film?
10. In *Home Alone*, who first realises Kevin is left behind and where are they?

Answers - Christmas Films

1. 1940s
2. Jack Skellington
3. Irving Berlin
4. Love is All Around by Wet, Wet, Wet
5. Will Ferrell
6. France
7. Jim Henson
8. Wham!
9. Three – Brian, John and Joel
10. His mum Kate, on the flight to Paris

Christmas Jokes (1)

Can you finish this Christmas joke and give us the punchline?

1. What do you call a 3 legged donkey?
2. What did Santa do when he went speed dating?
3. What do grumpy sheep say at Christmas?
4. What kind of photos do elves take?
5. What do you get when you cross a snowman and a vampire?
6. What is Santa's favourite pizza?
7. Who is never hungry at Christmas?
8. Why didn't the ghost go to the Christmas party?
9. Why did no one bid for Rudolph and Dasher on eBay?
10. What language does Santa speak?

Answers - Christmas Jokes (1)

1. A wonky
2. He pulled a cracker
3. Baaaaa humbug
4. Elfies
5. Frostbite
6. One that's deep and crisp and even
7. The turkey- he is always stuffed
8. He had no body to go with
9. They were two deer
10. North Polish

Christmas Anagrams

We've mixed up the letters of a popular Christmas item. Can you rearrange them to find the answer – be aware that some do have two words.

1. Cost King
2. My Niche
3. A Verdant Candle
4. Sea Bulb
5. Imp Niece
6. Heron Plot
7. Hermit Actress
8. Serpents

Answers - Christmas Anagrams

1. Stocking
2. Chimney
3. Advent Calendar
4. Baubles
5. Mince Pie
6. North Pole
7. Christmas Tree
8. Presents

Christmas True or False

Some Christmas facts now, but some are not true. Can you separate the fact from the fiction?

1. The traditional Christmas Pudding was originally a kind of soup, made from raisins and wine.
2. It was Pope Clement I that proclaimed December 25th the celebration date for Christ's birthday in 92 AD
3. In 1962 the first Christmas themed postage stamp was issued in the US
4. Christmas trees are grown and harvested in all 50 US states
5. In Ireland it is the tradition to leave out a mince pie and Guinness for Santa
6. Poinsettia is indigenous to Peru and was cultivated by the Incas
7. Abraham Lincoln was allegedly the first US President to have a Christmas tree at the White House
8. Christmas trees are typically sold by weight
9. Cranberries are grown on trees
10. The mistletoe was a sacred plant to the Druids

Answers - Christmas True or False

1. True - it was called Frumenty
2. False, it was Pope Julius I in 350 AD
3. True
4. True
5. True
6. False - it is indigenous to Mexico and was cultivated by the Aztecs
7. False - it is purported to have been Franklin Pierce (but see next section for more on this)
8. False - they are typically sold by height
9. False – they are grown on bushes in bogs!
10. True

Trivia - Christmas Trees at the White House

In the previous round we asked a question about the first US President to have a Christmas Tree at the White House. This is a surprisingly difficult question to answer - google it and you will come up with many different answers. In an attempt to answer this once and for all, we've come up with a chronology of Christmas Trees at the White House!

1800 - There wasn't a Christmas Tree yet, but the first Christmas Party at the White House was hosted by President John Adams and his wife Abigail, but it would have been much smaller and more intimate than the festivities of many later Presidents.

1853 - The 14th President, Franklin Pierce, decorated an evergreen tree on the White House lawn.

1889 - President Benjamin Harrison brought a Christmas Tree inside the White House and decorated it with lit candles.

1894 - When Grover Cleveland was President, electric Christmas lights adorned the White House Tree for the first time, much to the delight of his children.

1902 - Theodore Roosevelt was against cutting down a tree to decorate for Christmas, but his eight year old son did it anyway, hiding the tree in a closet!

1912 - The modern tradition has the White House Christmas Tree in the Blue Room, but it was in 1912 that President William H. Taft's children put a tree in the Blue Room for the first time.

1923 - Calvin Coolidge hosted the first Christmas Tree lighting ceremony at the White House.

1961 - There's something of a tradition of themed Christmas Tree decorations in the Blue Room, but this tradition was started by Jacqueline Kennedy in 1961 with decorated toys from the Nutcracker ballet.

Christmas Songs

Everyone loves a Christmas tune. Can you answer these questions about some Christmas favourites?

1. Which group sang *Little Saint Nick*?
2. Which Christmas song begins 'oh the weather outside is frightful, but the fire is so delightful'?
3. Which Christmas song refers to lords, ladies and pipers?
4. Which song was first performed in 1847 and has since been recorded by Mariah Carey, Celine Dion, Cher, Bing Crosby, Whitney Houston, Perry Como and Ellie Goulding?
5. Which well known carol is the story of a Czech king going to give alms to a poor man in winter?
6. *Happy Xmas (War is Over)* was a hit for which Liverpudlian singer?
7. *Have Yourself a Merry Little Christmas* was a hit for Judy Garland, but which film did it feature in?
8. Who famously sang with The Pogues on *Fairytale of New York?*
9. What famous Christmas Carol did Rector Phillips Brooks of Philadelphia write, inspired by an 1868 trip to the Holy Land?
10. What is the name of the famous snowman who has a song all about him, first recorded by Gene Autry in 1950?

Answers - Christmas Songs

1. The Beach Boys
2. Let It Snow, Let It Snow, Let It Snow
3. The 12 Days of Christmas
4. Holy Night
5. Good King Wenceslas
6. John Lennon
7. Meet Me in St Louis
8. Kirsty McCall
9. O Little Town of Bethlehem
10. Frosty

Christmas Books

Some books contain a little Christmas cheer. Can you answer these questions about a few?

1. *Hercule Poirot's Christmas* was written by which famous author?
2. How many ghosts appear in *A Christmas Carol*?
3. Who wrote *How the Grinch Stole Christmas*?
4. In *Little Women* by Louisa May Alcott, which character returns home from the American Civil War on Christmas Day?
5. Judith Kerr wrote a series of books about a cat, including a Christmas book published in 1976. What was the name of this feline?
6. *Sophie's World, The Solitaire Mystery* and *The Christmas Mystery* are all books by which Norwegian author?
7. Epic fantasy author J. R. R. Tolkien also wrote *Letters from Father Christmas,* but who were they written to?
8. Which director also wrote *The Nightmare Before Christmas*?
9. *The Gift of the Magi* is a short story written by which famous American author?
10. Which multiple *New York Times* bestselling thriller author also wrote *The Christmas Train*?

Answers - Christmas Books

1. Agatha Christie
2. Four – the ghosts of past, present and future as well as Jacob Marley
3. Dr. Seuss
4. Mr March, the girls' father
5. Mog
6. Jostein Gaarder
7. His children
8. Tim Burton
9. O. Henry (or William Sydney Porter)
10. David Baldacci

Playing Santa

Quite a few people have played Santa over the years. Can you identify these famous actors or actresses?

1. Who voiced Santa Claus in *The Polar Express*?
2. Which actor whose first main role was in TV show *Roseanne*, voiced Santa in *Futurama* in 1999 and *It's a Spongebob Christmas!* in 2012?
3. Who played an initially unwilling Santa in *The Santa Clause* in 1994 and its sequels?
4. *The Christmas Chronicles* 2018 features which actor as Santa Claus?
5. Which actress, better known for *Pitch Perfect* and *Twilight* played Noelle Kringle in 2019's *Noelle*?
6. Best known for his recurring role in the Harry Potter series, who was Santa in *A Muppets Christmas: Letter to Santa*?
7. Edmund Gwenn played Kris Kringle in the 1947 version and Richard Attenborough played him in the 1994 version, but what is the name of the film?
8. Ed Asner played Santa in which extremely popular film of 2003?
9. Which John, an American actor in over 70 films, also a director and producer, played Santa in *Santabear's High Flying Adventure* in 1987?
10. Which veteran actor born Ninnian Joseph Yule Jr in 1920, voiced Santa in *The Year Without a Santa Claus* in 1974 and *A Miser Brother's Christmas* in 2008?

Answers - Playing Santa

1. Tom Hanks
2. John Goodman
3. Tim Allen
4. Kurt Russell
5. Anna Kendrick
6. Richard Griffiths
7. *Miracle on 34th Street*
8. *Elf*
9. John Malkovich
10. Mickey Rooney

Favourite Pantomime Characters

If you have ever seen a pantomime then you have experienced something unique. Can you answer these questions about famous pantomime characters? Do not worry if you have never seen one as they are based on very well-known stories and tales.

1. Dick Whittington's cat rids London of which type of animal?
2. Snow White eats which poisoned fruit?
3. Which prince marries Cinderella at the end of the pantomime?
4. What are the names of Wendy's two brothers in Peter Pan?
5. What has Sleeping Beauty pricked her finger on that makes her go to sleep?
6. In which pantomime is 'Be Our Guest' a key song?
7. What animal does Jack sell to get the magic beans in Jack and the Beanstalk?
8. What is the name of Aladdin's brother who works in the laundry?
9. What kind of eggs does Priscilla the goose lay in Mother Goose?
10. In which pantomime does a dying miller leave the mill to his eldest son, a mule to his middle son and a cat to his youngest son?

Answers - Favourite Panto Characters

1. Rats
2. Apple
3. Prince Charming
4. John and Michael
5. A spinning wheel/ spindle
6. Beauty and the Beast
7. The cow
8. Wishy Washy
9. Golden eggs
10. Puss in Boots

Bestselling Christmas Toys

Every year there are certain toys that are the must-have for that year. Take a look at these questions and see if you can rekindle your childhood or that of your children.

1. What form changing plastic toy was a big hit in 1985?
2. A game about eating small plastic balls was popular in 1980 -what was it called?
3. *Furby Boom* was a big hit in 2013, but in what year had a Furby been the ultimate toy on a Christmas list?
4. A Nintendo creation topped the list in 2007, but which console was it?
5. The year before, 2006, had been a different console – which one this time?
6. 1977 and 2004 both saw the exact same product as the best-selling Christmas Toy. What was it?
7. What colourful gift topped the list in 1981?
8. Created by Japanese gaming company Epoch, which range of figurines were all the rage in 1987?
9. Which toy that hails from Denmark released a popular train in 1982?
10. Which toy that you have to remember to feed made the 1997 list?

Answers - Bestselling Christmas Toys

1. Transformers
2. Hungry Hippos
3. 2000
4. Nintendo Wii
5. Xbox 360
6. BMX Bike
7. Rubix Cube
8. Sylvanian Families
9. Lego – The Lego Train Set
10. Tamagotchi

Christmas History

Try these questions with a historical theme.

1. What is boxing day named after?
2. In what decade of the 1800s was the first Christmas Card sent?
3. Which US state last declared Christmas Day a holiday in 1907?
4. Who was crowned King of England on Christmas Day 1066?
5. What was gifted to the USA by the people of France in 1886 at Christmas?
6. Tinsel originated in Germany in 1610 and was originally spun from what?
7. Which fruit is the first documented decoration for Christmas tree?
8. Which popular Christmas song, was the first song played in space?
9. The word Xmas is actually an old word and dates back to which century?
10. Which well-known inventor created Christmas lights with friend Edward H. Johnson?

Answers - Christmas History

1. In Victorian times it was the day after Christmas Day when servants had a day off and were given a box of goodies from their employer to take to their family
2. 1840s (1843)
3. Oklahoma
4. William I "The Conqueror"
5. The Statue of Liberty
6. Silver
7. Apples
8. Jingle Bells
9. The 16th century (1500s)
10. Thomas Edison

Lyrics From Christmas Songs

Here are two lines from a Christmas song, all you need to do is name the song.

1. Dreams of Santa, dreams of snow/ Fingers numb, faces aglow
2. Free your mind of doubt and danger/ Be for real don't be a stranger
3. They hear a choir sing a song/ The music seemed to come from afar
4. There's a world outside your window/ And it's a world of dread and fear
5. Time for parties and celebration/ People dancing all night long
6. And I'm just gonna keep on waiting/ Underneath the mistletoe
7. With the kids jingle belling/ And everyone telling you be of good cheer
8. It'll be cold, so cold/ Without you to hold
9. Does he ride a red nosed reindeer/ Does he turn up on his sleigh
10. Thought I heard you say you love me/ That your love was gonna be here to stay

Answers - Lyrics From Christmas Songs

1. Mistletoe and Wine
2. 2 Become 1
3. Mary's Boy Child
4. Do They Know It's Christmas?
5. Merry Christmas Everyone
6. All I Want for Christmas is You
7. It's the Most Wonderful Time of the Year
8. Lonely This Christmas
9. Merry Christmas Everybody
10. Stay Another Day

Christmas Geography

Give these geography themed questions a go.

1. What ocean does Christmas Island lie in?
2. Name one of the two US states with towns called Santa Claus?
3. In November 2014, 1,762 people dressed as Santa's elves came together to make a new world record, in which Asian country?
4. In which island country is it popular to eat fried chicken on Christmas day?
5. In which country is Christmas morning first celebrated?
6. In which modern day country is Bethlehem?
7. Santa's workshop is in Lapland, but which country is it?
8. Bethlehem is a village in which country of the UK?
9. What is the snowiest country on earth?
10. Penguins are only found in one hemisphere but is it northern or southern?

Answers - Christmas Geography

1. The Indian Ocean
2. Indiana and Georgia. There was a third in Arizona, but it is a ghost town, abandoned in 1995.
3. Thailand
4. Japan
5. New Zealand (according to the Greenwich Observatory)
6. Palestine
7. Finland
8. Wales
9. Japan – Aomori City gets over 300 inches of snow some years!
10. Southern hemisphere

Who Am I? (1)

Eight clues to a famous person connected to Christmas. The quicker you get it, the better you do.

1. I am a parent

2. I make things for my work

3. I thought my girlfriend had cheated on me

4. I went on a long journey with my family

5. I have been called obedient and faithful

6. I came from Galilee

7. My wife was called Mary

8. My son was called Jesus

Answers - Who Am I? (1)

It is of course Joseph, wife of Mary and father of Jesus. Well, biologically not, spiritually not, but he (presumably) raised him…

Christmas Pot Luck

A mix of questions to get you thinking about Christmas.

1. What star sign are those born on Christmas Day?
2. What is the Christmas wreath a symbol for?
3. Mistletoe is popular around Christmas, but what colour are its berries?
4. The tradition of putting coal in the stocking of a naughty child at Christmas began in which country?
5. Name two of the three wise men.
6. Which saint took the tradition of wassailing and turned it into what we know as carolling?
7. Which kind of creature helps make toys in Santa's workshop at the North Pole?
8. What date do the twelve days of Christmas start on?
9. What is the highest grossing Christmas film of all time?
10. What was the mother of Baby Jesus called?

Answers - Christmas Pot Luck

1. Capricorn
2. The crown of thorns that Jesus wore
3. White
4. Italy
5. Caspar, Melchoir and Balthasar
6. St Francis of Assisi
7. Elves
8. 25th December
9. Home Alone
10. Mary

Christmas Carol Initials

We've given you the initials of some well-known Christmas carols. Can you guess the titles?

1. HTHAS
2. GRYMG
3. JTTW
4. DTH
5. ITBM
6. CC
7. ICUAMC
8. OIRDC
9. THATI
10. AFTROG
11. TFN
12. COTB
13. SN
14. OCAYF
15. AIAM

Answers - Christmas Carol Initials

1. Hark the Herald Angels Sing
2. God Rest Ye Merry Gentlemen
3. Joy To the World
4. Deck the Halls
5. In the Bleak Midwinter
6. Coventry Carol/ Calypso Carol
7. It Came Upon a Midnight Clear
8. Once in Royal David's City
9. The Holly and the Ivy
10. Angels From the Realms of Glory
11. The First Noel
12. Carol of the Bells
13. Silent Night
14. O Come All Ye Faithful
15. Away in a Manger

Christmas Word Ladder (1)

I've always loved word ladders. The idea is to transform one word into another, by changing one letter at a time. Each step has to be a real word. For instance to get from DOG to CAT, you would do something like DOG-DOT-COT-CAT. This one is slightly tricker than that example, but still fairly straightforward and using everyday words. Can you get from PINE to TREE?

PINE

_ _ _ _

_ _ _ _

_ _ _ _

_ _ _ _

_ _ _ _

_ _ _ _

_ _ _ _

_ _ _ _

TREE

You should be able to do it in 8 steps, not including PINE and TREE, but if you need more words don't worry.

Answers - Christmas Word Ladder (1)

This is just our suggested answer, there will be lots of different ones.

PINE

FINE

FILE

FILL

FELL

FEEL

FEET

FRET

FREE

TREE

Christmas Jokes (2)

Our second set of jokes. We've given you the question, can you guess the punchline?

1. What happens to elves when they are naughty?
2. What carol is heard in the desert?
3. What is Santa's favourite place to deliver presents?
4. What kind of motorbike does Santa ride?
5. How much did Santa pay for his sleigh?
6. What happened to the man who stole an advent calendar?
7. What do you get if you cross Santa with a duck?
8. The turkey's in a new band, but why does he have to play the drums?
9. Why did Santa get a parking ticket on Christmas Eve?
10. How do Christmas trees get ready for a night out?

Answers - Christmas Jokes (2)

1. Santa gives them the sack
2. O camel ye faithful
3. Idaho-ho-ho
4. A Holly Davidson
5. Nothing, it was on the house
6. He got 25 days
7. Christmas quacker
8. He's the only one with drumsticks
9. He left his sleigh in a no parking zone
10. They spruce up

Christmas Games

Games are popular at Christmas. Can you get the answers right to these game related questions?

1. Which game removed three of its playing pieces in 2017 and replaced them with a rubber ducky, penguin and T-Rex after an online vote?
2. Which game involves drawing a picture to enable your partner to guess the word on your card?
3. Ticket to Ride has sold more than how many copies worldwide? Is it 1 million, 3 million or 8 million?
4. Which game features round cards where you have to match one symbol with another card?
5. Which game involves placing certain body parts on coloured spots on the 'board'?
6. What game is subtitled 'A party game for horrible people.'?
7. In which game would you have a rope, a lead pipe and a candlestick?
8. Which games company focuses on children's games and makes Animal Upon Animal, Rhino Hero and Valley of the Vikings?
9. Which computer game series has the editions Ocarina of Time, Skyward Sword, Link's Awakening and Breath of the Wild?
10. What is exploding in the title of a popular Russian-roulette style game?

Answers - Christmas Games

1. Monopoly
2. Pictionary
3. 8 million
4. Dobble
5. Twister
6. Cards Against Humanity
7. Cluedo or Clue
8. Haba
9. Zelda
10. Exploding Kittens

Christmas Colours

All of these questions have a colour in the answer. Can you get them?

1. The film *Black Christmas* was released in what year of the 2010s?
2. What was the original colour of Father Christmas' suit?
3. What colour is a holly berry?
4. Which classic Christmas film of 1954 features Bing Crosby, Danny Kaye and Rosemary Clooney?
5. The symbolic Christingle used in advent is typically created using which fruit?
6. The three kings brought Baby Jesus frankincense, myrrh and what?
7. What coin was traditionally stirred into a Christmas pudding?
8. Which colourful song by Elvis Presley is right for the season?
9. Which plant, often known as The Christmas Flower, has large green leaves and red flowers?
10. Which Quality Street chocolate, now known by a colour, is a whole hazelnut in liquid caramel?

Answers - Christmas Colours

1. 2019
2. Green
3. Red
4. White Christmas
5. Orange
6. Gold
7. A silver sixpence
8. Blue Christmas
9. Poinsettia
10. The Purple One

Christmas TV Specials

Plenty of TV shows give us a special Christmas episode during the holidays. Can you get the answer right to these ones?

1. In the Friends episode 'The One with the Holiday Armadillo', who dresses up as the armadillo?
2. The West Wing episode 'In Excelsis Deo' was the Christmas special for which season?
3. In which 1996 sitcom's special, does the main character eat four Christmas dinners, take the shortest taxi ride ever and seemingly get proposed to by Peter Capaldi playing a BBC producer?
4. Which Seattle based show's first Christmas episode was titled 'Miracle on 3rd or 4th Street'?
5. In which show's Christmas special does the title character lose his watch in a turkey and then put his head inside it and walk around?
6. In which show's season six Christmas special written by Chris Carter, do the two main characters investigate a haunted house in Maryland?
7. Which pop star played Astrid Peth in the Christmas special of Doctor Who in 2007 with David Tennant?
8. Which two word animated show has Christmas specials titled 'Mr.Hankey, the Christmas Poo', 'Merry Christmas Charlie Manson!' and 'The Problem with a Poo'?
9. In the season six Cheers episode, 'Christmas Cheers', which character is working as a department store Santa?
10. In which show's only original Christmas special, does one of the title characters announce he'll be moving from Billericay in Essex to Barry in Wales in the New Year?

Answers - Christmas TV Series

1. Ross
2. Season One
3. The Vicar of Dibley
4. Frasier
5. Mr Bean
6. X-Files
7. Kylie
8. South Park
9. Norm
10. Gavin and Stacey

Who Am I? (2)

Eight more clues to a famous person linked to Christmas. Can you find the answer quicker than your friends and family?

1. I am the youngest child
2. My family are rich
3. I know right from wrong
4. I am handy with an iron
5. I made friends with Mr Marley
6. I like the film *Angels with Filthy Souls*
7. I never got to see Paris
8. I was left home alone

Answers - Who Am I? (2)

Kevin McCallister from *Home Alone*

Christmas Nativity

For Christians especially, the nativity story is an important part of Christmas. Can you get these right?

1. What was the name of the angel that told Mary she was having a baby?
2. Where did Mary and Joseph live?
3. What religion were Mary and Joseph when Jesus was born?
4. What animal does pregnant Mary travel to Bethlehem on?
5. Which King tried to have Jesus killed?
6. In which month does the Bible say that Jesus was born?
7. Who followed the star to find Jesus?
8. Where was Jesus laid after he was born?
9. Why was Jesus born in a stable instead of an inn?
10. Which prophet proclaimed that a virgin would give birth to a baby called Immanuel?

Answers - Christmas Nativity

1. Gabriel
2. Nazareth
3. Jewish
4. A donkey
5. Herod
6. It doesn't specify a month
7. The wise men
8. A manger
9. The inns were full and there was no room
10. The prophet Isaiah

The Twelve Days of Christmas

Can you name all of the gifts in the 12 days of Christmas song?

For a bonus point, how many gifts in total are received by the twelfth day. Bear in mind that gift number one is given on all 12 days, gift number two is given on 11 days etc.

Answers - The Twelve Days of Christmas

1. One partridge in a pear tree
2. Two turtle doves
3. Three french hens
4. Four calling birds
5. Five gold rings
6. Six geese-a-laying
7. Seven swans-a-swimming
8. Eight maids-a-milking
9. Nine ladies dancing
10. Ten lords-a-leaping
11. Eleven pipers piping
12. Twelve drummers drumming

And all the gifts make 364 in total.

Christmas Word Ladder (2)

A slightly trickier word ladder. Can you get from WINTER to JINGLE by changing one letter at a time? This time we've given you clues!

WINTER

_ _ _ _ _ _   Champion

_ _ _ _ _ _   Looking paler than usual

_ _ _ _ _ _   Slogan emblazoned across

_ _ _ _ _ _   You're forbidden to do this

_ _ _ _ _ _   ……. up – in prison?

_ _ _ _ _ _   Stuffed-up

_ _ _ _ _ _   A not for the faint-hearted jump

_ _ _ _ _ _   Clumsily attempted

_ _ _ _ _ _   George is of this

JINGLE

Answers - Christmas Word Ladder (2)

WINTER

WINNER

WANNER

BANNER

BANNED

BANGED

BUNGED

BUNGEE

BUNGLE

JUNGLE

JINGLE

Santa by Any Other Name

Santa is not simply Santa everywhere. In what language do they call Santa the following name/s?

1. Père Noël
2. De Kerstman
3. Babbo Natale
4. Papai Noel & Bom Velhinho
5. Saint Nick & Kris Kringle
6. Sinterklass or Kersvader
7. Ded Moroz or Grandfather Frost
8. Pai Natal
9. Daidí na Nollag
10. Julenisse

Answers - Santa by Any Other Name

1. France
2. Holland
3. Italy
4. Brazil
5. USA
6. South Africa
7. Portugal
8. Russia
9. Republic of Ireland
10. Norway

Christmas No. 1's

We'll give you the year and the artist, as well as the initials. All you need to do is name the song.

1. 1995, Michael Jackson – ES
2. 1961, Danny Williams – MR
3. 2019, Ladbaby – ILSR
4. 1987, Pet Shop Boys – AOMM
5. 2010, Matt Cardle – WWC
6. 1955, Dickie Valentine – CA
7. 1975, Queen – BR
8. 2006, Leona Lewis – AMLT
9. 1971, Benny Hill – E (TFMITW)
10. 1998, Spice Girls – G
11. 1964, The Beatles – IFF
12. 1980, St Winifred's School Choir - TNOQLG
13. 2002, Girls Aloud – SOTU
14. 1962, Elvis Presley – RTS
15. 2017, Ed Sheeran   - P

Answers - Christmas No. 1's

1. Earth Song
2. Moon River
3. I Love Sausage Rolls
4. Always On My Mind
5. When We Collide
6. Christmas Alphabet
7. Bohemian Rhapsody
8. A Moment Like This
9. Ernie (The Fastest Milkman in the West)
10. Goodbye
11. I Feel Fine
12. There's No One Quite Like Grandma
13. Sound of the Underground
14. Return to Sender
15. Perfect

Christmas Missing Vowels (2)

Harder than our original missing vowels round, we have moved around the consonants this time, so they are still in the correct order, but the word breaks are not in the right place. To make it easier though all the questions are about Christmas people or characters.

1. TH RW SMN
2. NG LG BRL
3. R D LP HTHR DN SR NDR
4. MR YND J SPH
5. MR SCLS
6. SN TSL VS
7. BB YJ SS
8. THG RN CH
9. LTT LD RMM RBY
10. FRS TYT H SN WMN

Answers - Christmas Vowels (2)

1. Three Wise Men
2. Angel Gabriel
3. Rudolph the Red Nose Reindeer
4. Mary and Joseph
5. Mrs Claus
6. Santas Elves
7. Baby Jesus
8. The Grinch
9. Little Drummer Boy
10. Frosty the Snowman

Name the Film By the Stars

Simply name the film by the list of some of the actors and actresses who are in it. They all feature in the top 50 grossing Christmas films of all time.

1. Kate Winslet, Cameron Diaz, Jude Law, Jack Black
2. James McAvoy, Hugh Laurie, Bill Nighy, Imelda Staunton
3. Vince Vaughn, Reese Witherspoon, Sissy Spacek, Mary Steenburgen
4. Arnold Schwarzenegger, Sinbad, Jim Belushi, Jake Lloyd
5. Emilia Clarke, Henry Golding, Michelle Yeoh, Emma Thompson
6. Billy Bob Thornton, Bernie Mac, Lauren Graham, Tony Cox
7. Vince Vaughn, Paul Giamatti, Miranda Richardson, Rachel Weisz
8. Tim Allen, Jamie Lee Curtis, Dan Aykroyd, Jake Busey
9. Bill Murray, Karen Allen, John Forsyth, Robert Mitchum
10. Danny DeVito, Matthew Broderick, Kristin Davis, Kristin Chenoweth

Answers - Name the Film By the Stars

1. *The Holiday*
2. *Arthur Christmas*
3. *Four Christmases*
4. *Jingle All the Way*
5. *Last Christmas*
6. *Bad Santa*
7. *Fred Claus*
8. *Christmas with the Kranks*
9. *Scrooged*
10. *Deck the Halls*

Christmas Trivia - Crackers

The Christmas Cracker is something of an essential for many people at Christmas, but how did they begin? They were actually invented by London based confectioner Tom Smith, who was inspired by a trip to Paris where he saw bon-bons wrapped in pretty coloured paper. As the crackers were typically given by men to ladies, he added short love poems on slips of paper - a precursor to the modern slip of paper with a corny joke on!

It was while he was sat by the fire listening to the crackling of logs that he came up with the idea for introducing a 'bang' - or so the story goes anyway. The 'bang' is created by a strip of paper inside the cracker coated with a very tiny amount of gunpowder (a mix of potassium nitrate, charcoal and sulpher). The friction when the cracker is pulled is enough to set off the bang, and the cardboard tube contains the (mini) explosion!

It was Tom Smith's son, Walter, who started the tradition of including paper hats inside crackers, and then small toys, experimenting with different ideas and themes. Before long they really took off and became the Christmas tradition they are today, with all manner of different types available. You can still buy Christmas Crackers from the Tom Smith Company too.

Interesting Fact - Crackers were originally known as 'cosaques', possibly after the Cossacks, who were known for riding on horseback and firing their guns into the air.

Winter Sports

Some sports are associated strongly with winter. Can you answer these sporting questions?

1. Alpine, Nordic and Telemark are all types of which winter sport?
2. Which winter sport is played with stones and brooms?
3. The Jamaican bobsleigh team features in which 1993 film with John Candy?
4. Where were the 2018 Winter Olympics held?
5. What position does the athlete put themselves in during the Skeleton ride?
6. Which sport was invented in the 1960s and was originally called snurfing?
7. What is the most typical breed of dog used for sledding, as portrayed in the film *Snow Dogs*?
8. What is the 'ball' used in Ice Hockey called?
9. The axel, the salchow and the toe loop are all jumps in which winter sport?
10. What is apres-ski?

Answers - Winter Sports

1. Skiing
2. Curling
3. *Cool Runnings*
4. PyeongChang, South Korea (locality or country accepted)
5. They lie face down
6. Snowboarding
7. Husky (Siberian Husky)
8. A puck
9. Ice skating
10. The fun socialising after a day on the slopes!

Who Am I? (3)

Another chance to identify someone related to Christmas by eight clues. See how quickly you can get this one.

1. I am a hard worker
2. I like my food
3. I have pets
4. I like to get dressed up in a suit
5. I get a lot of post
6. I prefer to give than receive
7. I'm an icon
8. I have elfish friends

Answers - Who Am I? (3)

It is of course, Santa, who else!

Name the Christmas Item

What follows is a basic description of a Christmas related item. See how many you can guess.

1. Thickened meat stock for a Christmas dinner
2. Strings of tiny bulbs
3. Red hat with white pom pom
4. The first thing on 25th December, in a church
5. Frozen water units shaped like a human
6. Prickly green plant used in circles
7. Sweet stick in red and white
8. Long sock pinned by the fire
9. Open topped vehicle to hold a large bag
10. Spicy home decorated with sweets

Answers - Name the Christmas Item

1. Gravy
2. Christmas lights
3. Santa hat
4. Midnight mass
5. Snowman
6. Holly
7. Candy Cane
8. Stocking
9. Sleigh
10. Gingerbread House

Christmas Tipples

Christmas drinks are an important part of festivities for some. See if this quiz gets you in the Christmas spirit.

1. What kind of alcohol is a snowball made with?
2. Which drink uses the phrase 'Holidays are Coming'?
3. Mulled wine is a favourite tipple at German Christmas markets where it is called what?
4. Eggnog typically features which spice grated on top, a seed indigenous to Indonesia?
5. A Sea Breeze cocktail features which fruit that is associated with Christmas?
6. What is unusual about the top of an Irish Coffee?
7. Kir Royale is a mix of champagne and which kind of fruit liqueur?
8. Which berry is the main flavour of gin?
9. In what decade was Babycham first released?
10. A Balthazar is a large bottle of champagne, but how much does it hold?

Answers - Christmas Tipples

1. Advocaat
2. Coca-Cola
3. Glühwein
4. Nutmeg
5. Cranberry
6. It features a layer of cream which floats on top of the coffee
7. Blackcurrant
8. Juniper
9. The 1950s
10. 12 litres or 16 regular bottles

A Little Latin Christmas

All of the Latin terms below are the word for a specific Christmas animal. To help you out we have given you the English names for the eight animals as well, you just need to match them up!

1. Equus Asinus
2. Meleagris
3. Ursus Maritimus
4. Erithacus Rubecula
5. Agnus
6. Spheniscidae
7. Perdix Perdix
8. Rangifer Tarandus

And the English names are:

a. Lamb
b. Donkey
c. Partridge
d. Reindeer
e. Turkey
f. Polar Bear
g. Robin
h. Penguin

Answers - A Little Latin Christmas

1. Donkey
2. Turkey
3. Polar Bear
4. Robin
5. Lamb
6. Penguin
7. Partridge
8. Reindeer

Christmas Trivia - Mince Pies

Did you know that mince pies have a long history? They are medieval in origin, and originally had savoury meat in them. The pies were a mix of sweet and savoury, with spices, honey and dried fruits commonly added (sugar was not widely available). The ingredients were expensive, so usually reserved for special feast days. The pies were often baked in a rectangular dish, so people came to associate them with the manger that baby Jesus was in. Before long, dough effigies of Jesus were added to the pies to make them more obviously religious.

There was a myth that Oliver Cromwell banned mince pies – and all thing Christmas – however this is not actually true. In the seventeenth century though, some puritans weren't happy at the idolatrous nature of the mince pies, so before the end of that century, the dough figure of baby Jesus had disappeared and the pies started to be made round. It wasn't until the 19th century that the meat started to be phased out in favour of the modern sweet mince pie however.

The Ultimate Christmas Quiz Book

Mince Pie Recipe

<u>Original Mince Pie Recipe</u>

The following is an ingredients list for a recipe for a mince pie which is taken from the medieval book, *A Book of Cookrye Very Necessary for All Delights Therin,* published in 1591. It is not quite complete however – can you fill in the ingredients from the information given?

For the filling:
1 1/2lb (700g) lean m_ _ _ _ _ or b_ _ _
4oz (100g) s_ _ _
1/2 tsp ground c_ _ _ _ _
1 tsp ground m_ _ _
1/2 tsp b_ _ _ _ p_ _ _ _ _
a pinch of s_ _ _ _ _ _
2oz (50g) r_ _ _ _ _ _
2oz (50g) c_ _ _ _ _ _ _
2oz (50g) stoned p_ _ _ _ _, chopped
For the pastry:
1lb (450g) plain f_ _ _ _
2tsps s_ _ _
4oz (100g) l_ _ _
1/4 pt (150ml) w_ _ _ _
4tbsp (60ml) m_ _ _
For the glaze:
1tbsp (15ml) b_ _ _ _ _
1tbsp (15ml) s_ _ _ _
1tbsp (15ml) r_ _ _w_ _ _ _

Answers - Mince Pie Recipe

For the filling:

1 1/2lb (700g) lean mutton or beef
4oz (100g) suet
1/2 tsp ground cloves
1 tsp ground mace
1/2 tsp black pepper
a pinch of saffron
2oz (50g) raisins
2oz (50g) currants
2oz (50g) stoned prunes, chopped

For the pastry:

1lb (450g) plain flour
2tsps salt
4oz (100g) lard
1/4 pt (150ml) water
4tbsp (60ml) milk
For the glaze:
1tbsp (15ml) butter
1tbsp (15ml) sugar
1tbsp (15ml) rosewater

Christmas Trivia - Song Royalties

In the film *About A Boy*, Hugh Grant's character is a singer who lives a comfortable bachelor lifestyle on the proceeds of a single bestselling Christmas song. Is this really possible? You may hear the same Christmas songs year in year out, but have you ever thought about how much it makes each year for the artists who sang them? Well in 2016, the British TV station Channel 5 did some research and it worked it out, coming up with the following (add 30% to 50% to convert to American dollars):

1. "Merry Xmas Everybody" by Slade £1m
2. "Fairytale of New York" by The Pogues and Kirsty MacColl £400,000
3. "All I Want for Christmas is You" by Mariah Carey £400,000
4. "White Christmas" by Bing Crosby £328,000
5. "Last Christmas" by Wham! £300,000
6. "Wonderful Christmastime" by Paul McCartney £260,000
7. "Stop the Cavalry" by Jona Lewie £120,000
8. "2000 Miles" by The Pretenders £102,000
9. "Mistletoe and Wine" by Cliff Richard £100,000
10. "Stay Another Day" by East 17 £97,000

Not bad for just one song eh?

Post Christmas Quizzes

Post-Christmas Trivia (1)

1. Which film won the Best Film Oscar 2021?
2. Which star sign covers mid-January to mid-February?
3. How many wives of Henry VIII were beheaded?
4. What is the currency of Denmark?
5. What is the largest planet in our solar system?
6. What is the name of the café everyone visits in the TV show *Friends*?
7. How many human players are there on the field in a game of polo?
8. What are pappardelle, linguine and orzo?
9. What is the meaning of the Latin phrase 'Veni, Vidi, Vici'?
10. What country of the world has the most miles of motorway?

Answers - Post-Christmas Trivia (1)

1. Nomadland
2. Aquarius
3. Two – Anne Boleyn and Katherine Howard
4. Danish Krone
5. Jupiter
6. Central Perk
7. Eight – four in each team
8. Types of pasta
9. I came, I saw, I conquered
10. China

Post-Christmas Trivia (2)

1. Who sang the songs Borderline, Live to Tell and Dear Jessie?
2. 'Just Do It' is the slogan of which sportswear company?
3. Wagyu or Kobe beef originates from which country?
4. What are the five colours of the Olympic rings?
5. What colour pill does Neo choose to swallow in The Matrix film?
6. In the Marvel franchise, which character is a living tree?
7. How many zeros are there in one million?
8. How many players are there in a football team (and soccer!)?
9. What in the human body is the patella?
10. Which 1977 Stephen King novel takes place at the Overlook Hotel?

Answers - Post-Christmas Trivia (2)

1. Madonna
2. Nike
3. Japan
4. Blue, Red, Yellow, Green, Black
5. Red
6. Groot
7. Six
8. Eleven
9. The kneecap
10. *The Shining*

Post-Christmas Trivia (3)

1. Who sings the theme tune to the 2021 Bond film *No Time to Die*?
2. What is the capital city of Australia?
3. In Harry Potter, what is the name of Harry's owl?
4. How many keys are there on a piano?
5. The scapula is a term for which part of the body?
6. NaCl is the chemical symbol of which everyday substance, used in cooking?
7. Which actress also known for *Enola Holmes*, plays character Eleven in *Stranger Things*?
8. In Doctor Who, the first ever episode aired the day after which tragic event in the USA?
9. Swiss, Raclette and Paneer are all types of what food?
10. Yo-Yo Ma and Julian Lloyd-Webber are both known for playing which instrument?

Answers - Post-Christmas Trivia (3)

1. Billie Eilish
2. Canberra
3. Hedwig
4. 88
5. The shoulder blade
6. Salt
7. Milly Bobby Brown
8. The Assassination of President JFK
9. Cheese
10. Cello

Post-Christmas Trivia (4)

1. Which author wrote *The Hunger Games* series of books?
2. Name two noble gases (or try for all seven if you like!)
3. In which sci-fi TV show is 'Danger, Will Robinson' a well-known phrase?
4. What is the capital of Bulgaria?
5. The number plate of a car in which film is OUTATIME?
6. Which scientist discovered pencillin?
7. Rory McIlroy is known for which sport?
8. In which country was renowned painter Frida Kahlo born?
9. In 1952, Albert Einstein was offered the Presidency of which country, was it Poland, Israel, the USA or New Zealand?
10. Shih Tzu, Afghan Hound and Chow Chow are all breeds of which animal?

Answers - Post-Christmas Trivia (4)

1. Suzanne Collins
2. Neon, Argon, Xenon, Radon, Helium, Krypton, Oganesson
3. *Lost in Space*
4. *Sofia*
5. *Back to the Future*
6. Alexander Fleming
7. Golf`
8. Mexico
9. Israel
10. Dog

Post-Christmas Trivia (5)

1. Where were the 2020 Summer Olympics (they ended up being in 2021!) held?
2. What is the currency of South Africa?
3. How many notes are there in a musical scale?
4. What is the name of the snowman in Disney's *Frozen* films?
5. Which planet has the most moons?
6. Which instrument does Lisa play in *The Simpsons*?
7. How many Grand Slam titles has Serena Williams won, is it 15, 21 or 23?
8. Which island group includes Majorca, Menorca and Ibiza?
9. A DNA molecule is described as a certain double shape- what is it?
10. In Games of Thrones, what is the name of the youngest Stark child?

Answers - Post Christmas Trivia (5)

1. Tokyo, Japan
2. South African Rand
3. Seven
4. Olaf
5. Saturn
6. The saxophone
7. 23 – only one person has ever won more, Australian Margaret Court
8. The Balearics
9. Double helix
10. Rickon

Post-Christmas Link Words

A Post-Christmas link words while you work off those mince pies! One word can be added to these three to make three new words, but what word is it?

1. Adder, Pastry, Powder
2. Band, Plant, Stamp
3. Panther, Baby, Tickled
4. Ice, Steam, Iron
5. Line, Hive, Busy
6. China, Funny, Fracture
7. Pot, Spoon, Cup
8. Due, Estimate, Time
9. Nine, Hair, King
10. Opera, Box, Stone

Answers - Post Christmas Link Words

1. Puff
2. Rubber
3. Pink
4. Age
5. Bee
6. Bone
7. Tea
8. Over
9. Pin
10. Soap

Turn over to find out about some of our other great books.

All of our books are available for sale on Amazon.

A family puzzle book with classic puzzles like Wordsearch, Crossword and Sudoku along with lots of different varieties like Word Trees, Cryptograms, Mazes, Memory puzzles and lots more. Great for all ages from 7 and upwards.

The perfect quiz book for music lovers of all ages, this has rounds on lots of different artists, musical genres and decades as well as fun rounds like song blanks and misheard lyrics.

Part quiz book part puzzle book, this has everything from Anagrams to Cryptograms, Wordle style puzzles to Word ladders and lots more. Great for doing on your own or with friends, this is a great gift for fans of word games everywhere!

A bumper film quiz book with over 500 questions and rounds on Marvel, James Bond, Harry Potter and lots more. There's Famous Last Lines, Decades rounds, Give Us a Clue, Find the Links and plenty more.

This is a book stuffed full with 75 rounds of our famous Who What Where quizzes. Each round there's a famous person, place or thing to guess and 12 clues. How many clues will it take you to guess? Great for parties and with friends.

The ultimate book for keeping kids entertained on long car journeys or endless school holidays. These riddles are such fun, and kids enjoy showing the adults in their life how smart they really are!

Printed in Great Britain
by Amazon